Juggling Your Finances: Basic Excel Guide

M.L. HUMPHREY

Copyright © 2015, 2018 M.L. Humphrey

All rights reserved.

ISBN: 1725018411
ISBN-13: 978-1725018419

Originally published as Jugging Your Finances: Basic Excel Primer in a 8.5" x 11" size under ISBN 1511523255

TITLES BY M.L. HUMPHREY

BUDGETING FOR BEGINNERS
Budgeting for Beginners
Excel for Budgeting

EXCEL ESSENTIALS
Excel for Beginners
Intermediate Excel
50 Useful Excel Functions

WORD ESSENTIALS
Word for Beginners
Intermediate Word

POWERPOINT ESSENTIALS
PowerPoint for Beginners

WRITING ESSENTIALS
Writing for Beginners
Excel for Writers
Achieve Writing Success

SELF-PUBLISHING ESSENTIALS
Excel for Self-Publishers
AMS Ads for Authors
CreateSpace for Beginners
ACX for Beginners

CONTENTS

Introduction	1
Understanding Some Excel Basics	5
Addition Overview	15
Addition Examples	27
Subtraction Overview	37
Subtraction Examples	41
Multiplication Overview	49
Multiplication Examples	53
Division Overview	61
Division Examples	67
Excel Formatting and Navigation Tips and Tricks	75
Conclusion	97

INTRODUCTION

The purpose of this guide is to discuss how to use Excel for basic budgeting calculations. If you're a little rusty on basic math (addition, subtraction, multiplication, and division) then read the *Juggling Your Finances: Basic Math Guide* first.

This guide will walk through the same calculations as that one, but talk about how to use Excel to make the calculations as opposed to a calculator.

If you're familiar with Excel or don't plan on using it for budgeting, then you don't need to read this guide.

The guide will walk through how to do the following calculations in Excel.

Addition:
- Total income.
- Total expenses.
- Total balance in your accounts if you have multiple accounts.
- Total amount you owe if you have more than one credit card, loan, etc.

Subtraction:
 • How much money will be left over after you pay your bills.
 • Your net worth or liquid net worth. (In other words, how much you'd be worth if you sold everything you own and paid off everything you owe. The first one, net worth, is how much you're worth in theory, the second one, liquid net worth, is how much you're worth in reality.)
 • How much of a shortfall you might have if you're spending more than you earn.

Multiplication:
 • How much you'll earn when you know the rate you'll be paid per hour or task.
 • Your net earnings (how much you actually take home) from your gross earnings (how much you earn before taxes are taken out).
 • Your annual earnings or expenses based upon one month's earnings or expenses.

Division:
 • How much you earn or spend on average.
 • How many hours you need to work to earn a certain gross amount.
 • How much you need to gross in order to take home a certain net amount.
 • How many months of expenses you can cover with the current amount of cash you have in the bank.

In order to make it as easy as possible to learn the basics of using Excel for addition, subtraction, multiplication, and division, the main chapters focus only on how to do those mathematical computations. However, if you work in Excel to any great extent you will quickly find that you need to perform a number of other tasks such as widening columns, bolding text, and formatting text.

The Tips and Tricks chapter at the end covers these other functions in Excel. You'll likely refer to it often as you work through this guide and when I use a trick that's covered in that section I'll let you know.

This will probably seem pretty daunting at first, but just keep working with it and practicing and you'll quickly be able to perform any computation you want in Excel with ease.

As I mentioned in the *Basic Math Guide*, it's a really, really good idea to be comfortable enough with math that you can at least judge whether an answer makes any sense or not. A spreadsheet is only as good as the person creating and using it. If you put in the wrong information or set up a formula wrong, you will get a wrong answer.

Excel is just a tool and you need to know enough to understand when the tool isn't working properly.

Okay, enough of that.

Ready?

Let's get started.

UNDERSTANDING SOME EXCEL BASICS

Before we start, I want to make sure we're using the same terms. This is what Excel looks like when I first open it.

I'm working in Excel 2007, which is VERY different from earlier versions of Excel in terms of how it looks. Your basic math functions are pretty much the same, but the menus up top are completely different. If you're working in an earlier version and just now trying to learn Excel, I'd recommend that you upgrade your version of Excel. They're different enough that you really don't want to have to learn the newer version later.

But I'll try to keep this at a level that can work with any version of Excel, because your basic formulas really haven't changed across versions. Sometimes, though, that won't be possible. Especially when we talk about using the tabs at the top of the page to find the various options.

So, let's start by going over the terms I'll use throughout the rest of the guide.

Column

Excel uses columns and rows to display information. Columns run across the top of the worksheet and, unless you've done something funky with your settings, are identified using letters of the alphabet. As you can see below, they start with A on the far left side and march right on through the alphabet (A, B, C, D, E, etc.). If you scroll far enough to the right, you'll see that they continue on to a double alphabet (AA, AB, AC, etc.).

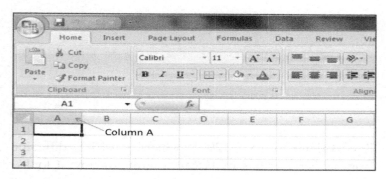

Row

Rows run down the side of the worksheet and are numbered starting at 1 and up to a very high number that will not matter for what you're doing here.

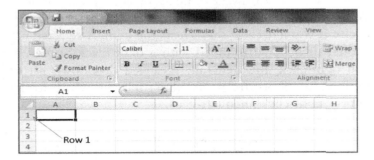

Cell

A cell is a combination of a column and row that is identified by the letter of the column it's in and the number of the row it's in. When you've clicked on a specific cell it will have a darker black border around the edges. Directly above you can see that for Cell A1 the border only shows on the bottom and right side. (See next page for image pointing to Cell A1.)

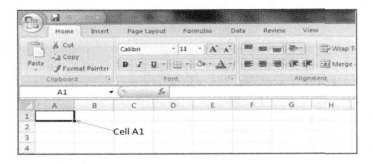

Click

If I tell you to click on something that means to use your mouse (or trackpad) to move the arrow on the screen over to a specific location and left-click or right-click on either the cell or tab or menu option. (See the next definition for the difference between left-click and right-click). If you left-click, this selects the item. A selected cell should then be surrounded with a dark black border. If you right-click, this generally creates a dropdown list of options to choose from. If I don't tell you which to do, left- or right-click, then left-click.

Left-click/Right-click

If you look at your mouse or your trackpad, you generally have two flat buttons to press. One is on the left side, one is on the right. If I say left-click that means to press down on the button on the left. If I say right-click that means press down on the button on the right. (If you're used to using Word or Excel you may already do this without even thinking about it. So, if that's the case then think of left-click as what you usually use to select text or options and right-click as what you use to see a menu of other choices.)

Spreadsheet

I'll try to avoid using this term, but if I do use it, I'll mean your entire Excel file. It's a little confusing because it can sometimes also be used to mean a specific worksheet, which is why I'll try to avoid it as much as possible.

Worksheet

This is the term I'll use as much as possible. A worksheet is basically a combination of rows and columns that you can enter data in. When you open an Excel file, it opens to worksheet one.

My version of Excel has three worksheets available by default when I open a new Excel file. (It's possible to add more as needed.) In my version, the worksheets are labeled Sheet 1, Sheet 2, and Sheet 3, and the one highlighted in white is the one I'm using at that moment. (See the Tabs definition below for a picture.)

Formula Bar

This is the long white bar at the top of the screen with the $f\chi$ symbol next to it. If you click in a cell and start typing, you'll see that what you type appears not only in that cell, but in the formula bar. When you enter a formula into a cell and then hit enter, the value returned by the formula will be what displays in the cell, but the formula will appear in the formula bar when you have that cell highlighted.

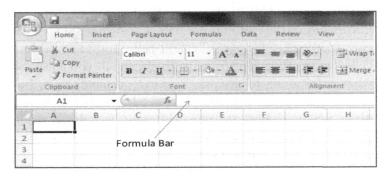

Tab

I use this term to refer to two separate things that work the same way.

One, as you saw above in the definition for a worksheet, I refer to the Sheet 1, Sheet 2, and Sheet 3 worksheets as tabs. Also, I refer to the menu choices, Home, Insert, Page Layout, Formulas, Date, Review and View, at the top of the page as tabs. Note how they look like folder tabs from an old-time filing system? That's why.

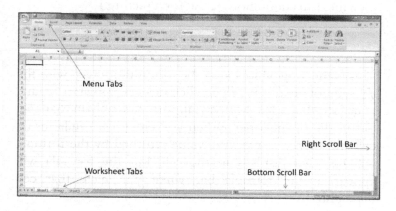

Each menu tab you select will show you different information. On my Home tab I can do things like copy/cut/paste, format cells, edit cells, and insert/delete cells, for example. This is really the main tab you'll use for what we're going to discuss. You can get fancy later, but most of the basics are here on this tab. (Note this is one place where things are very different for those using earlier versions of Excel and why if you're using an older version of Excel, I'd recommend upgrading now.)

Just as with the tabs across the top, each tab you select on the bottom shows you the contents of the selected worksheet.

Scroll Bar

I doubt this will come up here, but it's important to realize what the scroll bars are and how they work. See the image above under the definition of Tab. On the right side and the bottom of the screen are two bars with arrows at the ends. If you left-click and hold on either bar you can move it back and forth between those arrows (or up and down for the one on the right side). This lets you see information that's off the page in your current view but part of the worksheet you're viewing. You can also use the arrows at the ends of the scroll bar to do the same thing. Left-click on the arrow once to move it one line or column or left-click and hold to get it to move as far as it can go. Using the arrows instead of the clicking on the scroll bar will let you scroll all the way to the far end of the spreadsheet. The scroll bars will only let you move to the end of your information.

Data

I use data and information interchangeably. Whatever information you put into a worksheet is your data.

Select

If I tell you to "select" cells, that means to highlight them. If the cells are next to each other, you can just left-click on the first one and drag the cursor (move your mouse or finger on the trackpad) until all of the cells are highlighted. When this happens, they'll all be surrounded by a dark black box like below.

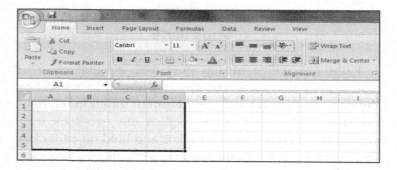

If the cells aren't next to each other, then what you do is left-click on the first cell, hold down the Ctrl key (bottom left of my keyboard), left-click on the next cell, hold down the Ctrl key, left-click on the next cell, etc. until you've selected all the cells you want. The cells you've already selected will be shaded in gray and the one you selected last will be surrounded by a black border that is not as dark as the normal black border you see when you've just selected one cell. In the image below cells A1, B2, C3, and B4 are selected.

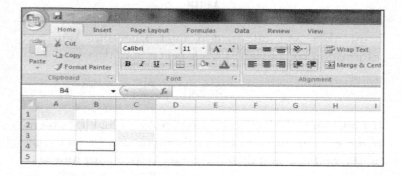

Cursor

If you didn't know this one already, it's what moves around when you move the mouse (or use the trackpad). In Excel it often looks like a three-dimensional squat cross or it will look like one of a couple of varieties of arrow. The different shapes you see mean that different functions are available at that time. We'll cover that later if you end up needing it.

Arrow

If I say that you can "arrow back" to something that just means to use the arrow keys to navigate from one cell to another. For example, if you enter information in A1 and hit enter, that moves your cursor down to cell A2. If you now want to go back to cell A1, you can just use the up arrow. (You can also just left-click in A1. It does the same thing.)

ADDITION: OVERVIEW

In this section we'll talk about the different ways in which you can add values in Excel. The next section will walk through some examples using basic budget-related calculations.

There are four ways you can add values in Excel.

Option 1: Put The Entire Formula In A Cell

First, you can just type the formula into any cell and hit enter.

To use a formula in Excel you need to START with the = sign. (As opposed to most calculators where you put it at the end.)

So, for example, if I wanted to add 15, 45, and 35, I could start typing in the cell I'm already in or left-click on a different cell and enter the following into the cell:

$$=15+45+35$$

When you hit enter, the cell should show you the value 95.

If you then arrow back up to the cell you just used, you'll see the formula (=15+45+35) in the formula bar above the spreadsheet and the value (95) in the cell

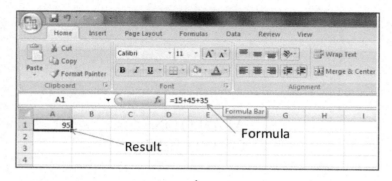

Sometimes you might screw up when you're entering things into Excel and it'll start doing weird things like selecting cells you didn't tell it to select and if you try to arrow back to correct it, it just selects other cells. (Or does that only happen to me?) If this happens, just hit the Esc key on your keyboard. It works a bit like an undo key by getting you out of whatever you're doing at that moment.

Usually what I described above happens when you're typing in a formula like =15+45+ and you then click in a different cell. Since Excel lets you include values from cells in your formulas, Excel thinks that's what you're trying to do and puts the location of the cell in the formula. Using the arrow keys at that point just results in Excel changing the cell name it's putting into the formula.

If those last two paragraphs didn't make sense to you, don't worry about it. One day they will or you'll never run across that particular issue and you won't need them. I just didn't want anyone getting hung up here because of an issue like that.

JUGGLING YOUR FINANCES: BASIC EXCEL GUIDE

So, remember, hit Esc if things are going wrong. Or Ctrl+Z (hold down the Ctrl key and the Z key at the same time) to undo the last thing you did if it's wrong.

Option 2: Select (or Highlight) the Cells You Want to Add

Your second option is to simply highlight the cells that you want to add together.

Let's say that your worksheet already has the amounts you want to add together. For example, A1 has 15, A2 has 45, and A3 has 35.

Select all three cells. (Left-click in A1 or A3 and move the cursor until all three cells are selected/highlighted. If you start with A2, you're going to have to use the Ctrl key to select all three cells because you can only click and move in one direction or the other.)

After you've selected the cells, you can take your hand off the mouse or trackpad and the cells should still be selected. You'll know they are because they'll be surrounded by a dark black border.

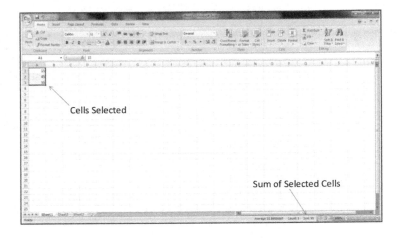

17

In the bottom right corner of the worksheet (below the scroll bar) you should see: Average, Count, and Sum with values listed after each one. This is the average, count, and sum of the values you have highlighted. In this case, your average is 31.66666667, your count is 3, and your sum is 95.

This means that you selected three cells (count of 3), that the total value in those cells was 95 (sum of 15, 45, and 35), and that the average of the three values was 31.67.

If you don't see Sum as one of your options, then, at least in later versions of Excel, right-click where it should say Average, Count, and Sum and you can customize what Excel refers to as the Status Bar. For example, I could also have it display Numerical Count, Minimum, and Maximum. If Sum isn't already checked, you just left-click on the left side of the word on the list and a check should appear. That will make it appear as an option in the bar at the bottom of the screen.

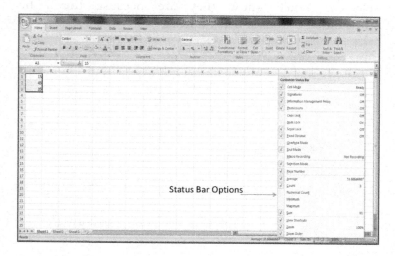

Status Bar Options

JUGGLING YOUR FINANCES: BASIC EXCEL GUIDE

Keep in mind that you'll only see the information at the bottom of the screen (average, count, sum) when you have more than one cell selected and those cells contain information.

Option 3: Use the AutoSum Button

This one requires you to have the values already entered somewhere in the spreadsheet. It also requires that they are either all in one row or all in one column. (Technically, you could use AutoSum and then change the formula to anything you want, but, really, we don't need to go there right now.)

The AutoSum button on my version of Excel is on the Home tab in the top right corner. It looks like a pointy uppercase E (the sum function from math) and has the words AutoSum next to it.

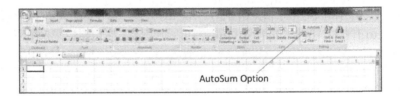
AutoSum Option

If the values are all in one column, (so, say in cells A1, A2, and A3) then click in the cell right below them (A4) and hit the AutoSum button. It should highlight all three cells with a dotted line and show a formula in cell A4.

Hit enter and you should see 95 in cell A4. If you click on A4, you'll see the following formula:

=SUM(A1:A3)

That means sum cells A1 through A3.

If the values are in one row (so, say in cells A1, B1, and C1) then click in the cell on the right side of the values (D1) and click on AutoSum. Same thing should happen. Cells A1, B1, and C1 are highlighted and it shows a formula. If you hit enter you'll see a value of 95 in cell D1. When you click back in cell D1 you'll see the following formula in the formula bar:

=SUM(A1:C1)

JUGGLING YOUR FINANCES: BASIC EXCEL GUIDE

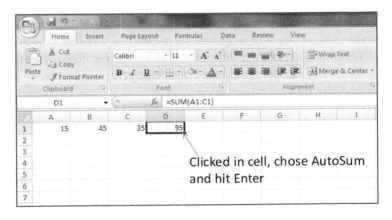

Clicked in cell, chose AutoSum and hit Enter

The key to using AutoSum is making sure that the AutoSum function actually selects all of the cells that you want it to. If there's a gap in your numbers, so a blank column or row, Excel will generally only select the cells prior to the gap. So, if you had values in cells A1, B1, and C1 and then D1 was blank and you had values in E1 and F1, when you click on AutoSum from cell G1, it's only going to select values from cells E1 and F1.

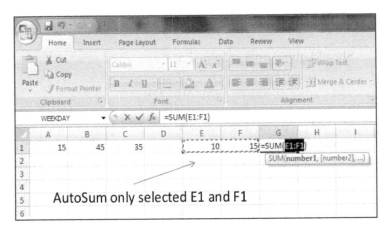

AutoSum only selected E1 and F1

(This is where being able to at least guesstimate what a value should be will help you tremendously. It lets you do a reality check on the numbers you're seeing. Remember, a worksheet is only as accurate as the person who creates it and the person who uses it.)

Option 4: Enter Your Own Formula

This is where it gets scary, right? Entering your own formula? But sometimes that's the easiest way to do things. And, once you get comfortable with Excel, it'll be what you do most of the time.

The basic Excel formula for adding things together is:

$$=SUM(\ )$$

Where what you put in the parens is what gets added together

If you use a comma, that means that each item is separate and distinct. So,

$$=SUM(2,3)$$

Should give you a result of 5.

$$=SUM(2,3,4)$$

Should give you a result of 9.

Honestly, if you're dealing with numbers like that, just use =2+3+4 in the cell instead. But a lot of times you'll be referencing cells like the AutoSum function did above and you'll have a whole row or column of cells that you want to add at once. That's when the SUM function has real power.

JUGGLING YOUR FINANCES: BASIC EXCEL GUIDE

Before we go through some examples, you need one more piece of information:

As you saw above, Excel uses the colon sign, : , in its formulas. Think of the colon sign as meaning "through." So, if I say A1:A5, that means cells A1, A2, A3, A4, and A5. If I say, A1:B2 that means cells A1, A2, B1, and B2.

That little colon is what lets you add a bunch of cells together with ease.

Remember how you had your values in cells A1, A2 and A3 and you highlighted them and glanced down at the bottom corner to see what they equaled?

Well, you could just as easily go to any cell in the spreadsheet and type:

=SUM(A1:A3)

You'd get the exact same result.

Now, just to make it even more confusing, you can start typing your formula and then select the cells you want to include with your mouse or trackpad.

Go to any cell, and type

=SUM(

and then select the cells you want to add together (left-click and drag for cells next to each other or left-click and use Ctrl for cells that aren't next to each other).

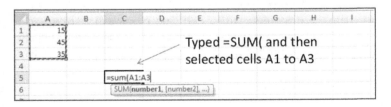

Excel will automatically write the formula for you using the cell names.

Once you've chosen all the cells you want, just type in the closing paren

)

and hit enter. You should see the value of all of the cells you selected added together in the cell and can click on it to see the formula in the formula bar.

If you're not sure you chose the right cells, double left-click in the cell with your formula. If the cells are next to each other, it will highlight them in a blue box.

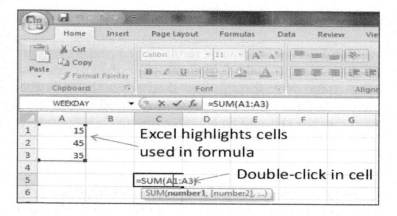

If they're not next to each other then each cell will be outlined with a different color and in the formula you see in the worksheet the cell names will show the corresponding color for each one. So, cell A3 will be green and so will the name A3 in the formula in the cell.

JUGGLING YOUR FINANCES: BASIC EXCEL GUIDE

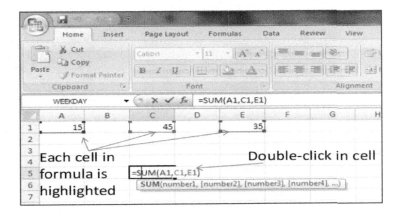

(After you double left-click in a box with a formula like this is when that Esc trick can come in very handy. If you've just double left-clicked on a formula and you click anywhere else before getting out of that cell by either hitting Enter or Esc, you'll accidentally select a new cell to put in the formula.)

* * *

So that's addition. There are four ways you can go about it.

Now let's walk through some examples using the types of calculations you'll want to perform to get a handle on your finances.

ADDITION: EXAMPLES

Example 1A: How much did you earn from housesitting this month?

Example 1B: How much did you earn total?

First, let's go over the information we used in the math guide, starting with your income for a given month. Let's say you:

- Housesit three times last month and were paid $25, $40, and $35.
- You also earned $52.23 from your retail job.
- And you were paid $10, $8, and $12 for dogwalking.

Step 1: Input the Information Into Excel

First step is to put all this information into a worksheet in Excel. Personally, I tend to include more information than I think I'll need, because I find it easier to input it all up front than have to go back later and add it in when I decide I need it.

So, open Excel and input the information into the first available worksheet.

This is what the first few rows of my worksheet look like after I've entered the information above:

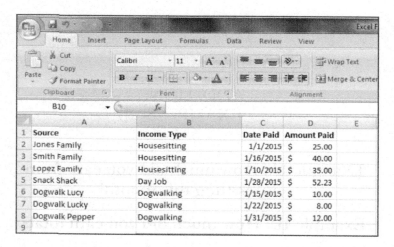

As you can see, I used Row 1 to name my columns. In this case I have four columns called Source, Income Type, Date Paid, and Amount Paid. I did this by clicking in each cell and typing in the text I wanted to see.

I recommend always using the top row to name your columns and trying to limit your headers to just that one row. I am a big fan of using the filter function in Excel, but it doesn't work well if you use more than one row for your column headers.

(Of course, the filter function works better the more recent the Excel version you're working in. Another reason to consider upgrading if you're using an older version of Excel.)

JUGGLING YOUR FINANCES: BASIC EXCEL GUIDE

What I did above looks simple, but there are a number of tricks I used to make it look like it does.

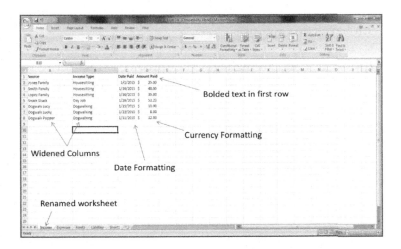

I don't want to distract from the basic math functions we're trying to learn here, but each of these steps is discussed in detail in the tips and tricks section at the end of the book under the headings: Date Formatting, Currency Formatting, Bolding Text, Renaming A Worksheet, and Widening Columns.

As a matter of fact, if this is the first time you've worked in Excel, I'd recommend reading through that section once now just to get familiar with what you can do in Excel besides the basic math functions we're discussing here.

Okay. Back to the example. So, we entered our information into Excel. What next?

Step 2: Add Your Numbers

Now you can use the different ways to add values that we discussed in the last chapter.

Example 1A: How much did you earn from housesitting this month?

You have two options:

Option 1. You can highlight the three cells that relate to housesitting and look at the value in the bottom right corner.

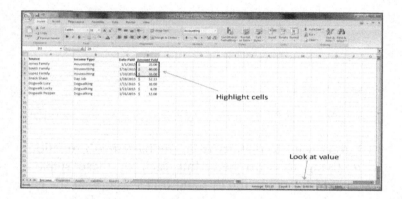

This is the best approach for when you just want a quick answer and won't need to see the result each time you open the worksheet.

Option 2. You can type a formula into any cell that doesn't already contain information and add the values related to housesitting:

=SUM(D2:D4)

JUGGLING YOUR FINANCES: BASIC EXCEL GUIDE

	A	B	C	D
				D11 =SUM(D2:D4)
1	Source	Income Type	Date Paid	Amount Paid
2	Jones Family	Housesitting	1/1/2015	$ 25.00
3	Smith Family	Housesitting	1/16/2015	$ 40.00
4	Lopez Family	Housesitting	1/10/2015	$ 35.00
5	Snack Shack	Day Job	1/28/2015	$ 52.23
6	Dogwalk Lucy	Dogwalking	1/15/2015	$ 10.00
7	Dogwalk Lucky	Dogwalking	1/22/2015	$ 8.00
8	Dogwalk Pepper	Dogwalking	1/31/2015	$ 12.00
9				
10	**Formula**	**Result**		
11		Housesitting Income		$ 100.00
12				

Note that I used the cell names (D2, D3, and D4) and not the numeric values in the formula. That's because if you use the values and later change one your formula will now be wrong.

For any worksheet you plan to use on an ongoing basis, you should always put your numeric values in cells in the spreadsheet and then write your formulas so they refer to those cells. That way you enter values once, use them many times. As much as possible, try not to include fixed values within any formulas.

If you take this approach, then you'll be able to easily see what assumptions or numbers are built into your calculations and you'll be able to change them quickly. Also, you can use the value in one cell for multiple calculations. (We'll go through a few examples later in the multiplication section.)

Either way, you should get $100 as your answer.

Also note that I didn't use the AutoSum option here. That's because you earned income from dog walking and your retail job as well as housesitting. If you used the AutoSum function at the bottom of your income entries, you'd be adding all of your sources of income, not just those for housesitting.

Example 1B: How much did you earn total?

You can use either of the options we used above.
   1. Highlight the cells and look at the value in the bottom corner.
   2. Enter a formula in any cell. In this case:

$$=SUM(D2:D8)$$

Or,

Option 3. You can use the AutoSum button in cell D9.

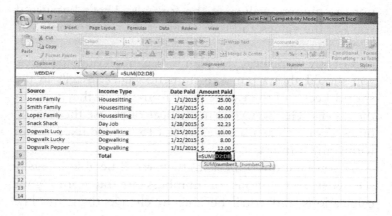

Whichever way you do it, you should get $182.23 as your answer.

Example 2: How much did you spend this month?

Going back to the math guide, we assumed you had the following expenses for the month:

JUGGLING YOUR FINANCES: BASIC EXCEL GUIDE

- Rent of $500
- Car insurance of $125
- Utilities of $75
- Credit card of $425

Step 1: Input the Information Into Excel

I did this in a new worksheet that I called Expenses. It looks like this:

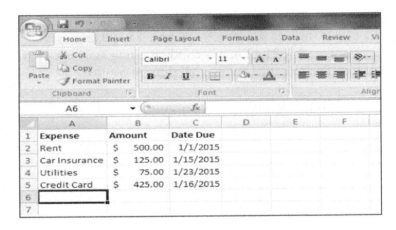

As before, I named the worksheet, bolded the text, widened columns, formatted dates, and formatted currency.

Step 2: Add It Up

You have three choices for adding the amounts:

1. Highlight the cells in column B and look in the bottom right corner for the value.
2. Enter a formula anywhere in the worksheet that adds those four cells. In this case:

=SUM(B2:B5)

3. Use AutoSum in cell B6

Whichever way you do it, you should get $1,125 as your answer.

Example 3: What is the total balance available in your accounts?

According to the math guide we assumed you have $1,542.21 in one checking account, $3,500 in a savings account, and $921.42 in a second checking account. How do you find the total value in all three accounts?

Step 1: Input the Information Into Excel

I did this in a new worksheet that I called Assets.
It looks like this:

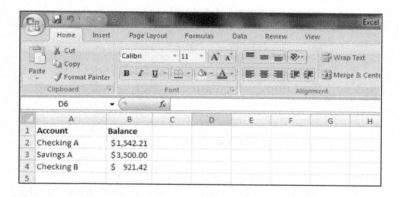

Step 2: Add It Up

You have three choices for adding the amounts:

1. Highlight the cells in column B and look in the bottom right corner for the value.
2. Enter a formula anywhere in the worksheet that adds those three cells. In this case:

=SUM(B2:B4)

3. Use AutoSum in cell B5

Whichever way you choose, you should get $5,963.63 for your total balance.

Example 4: What is the total amount you owe?

This is always a painful one to calculate, especially if you've just been blindly paying minimum payments and not looking at the total balance owed.

Same as above, of course.

Using the figures we used in the math guide, you have one student loan in the amount of $8,432.21, another in the amount of $4,563.78, a credit card in the amount of $473.99, and another credit card in the amount of $3,789.21.

Step 1: Input the Information Into Excel

I did this in a new worksheet that I called Liabilities.
It looks like this:

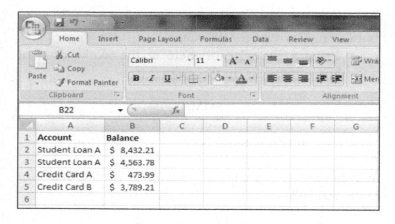

Step 2: Add It Up

You have three choices for adding the amounts:

1. Highlight the cells in column B and look in the bottom right corner for the value.

2. Enter a formula anywhere in the worksheet that adds those four cells. In this case:

$$=SUM(B2:B5)$$

3. Use AutoSum in cell B6

Whichever way you choose, you should get $17,259.19 for your total amount owed.

* * *

There you have it. Don't forget to review the tips and tricks section once you have the basics down so you can format your spreadsheet properly.

SUBTRACTION: OVERVIEW

There are really only two ways to subtract values in Excel.

Option 1: Put The Entire Formula In A Cell

First, you can just enter the formula into any cell and hit enter.

Just the same as with addition, in Excel you need to START with the = sign. (As opposed to most calculators where you put it at the end.)

So, for example, if I wanted to subtract 35 from 45, I could start typing in the cell I'm already in or left-click on a different cell and enter the following into the cell:

=45-35

When you hit enter, the cell should show you the value 10. If you then arrow back up to the cell you just used, you'll see the formula (=45-35) in the formula bar above the spreadsheet and the value (10) in the cell.

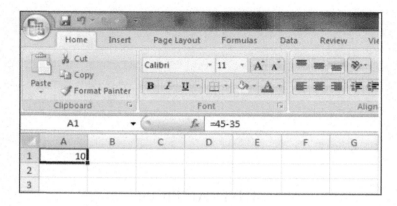

As with addition, remember that the Esc key and Ctrl+Z are your friends if something doesn't work the way you think it should. Esc gets you out of whatever you're doing. Ctrl+Z undoes the last thing you did (in most cases).

Just back up and try it again if it doesn't work the first time.

Option 2: Enter Your Own Formula

As with addition, sometimes this is the easiest way to do things. There isn't an equivalent to the SUM function for subtraction. You just put the minus sign, - , between each of the cells.

The basic Excel formula for subtracting things is:

$$=(\ )-(\ )-(\ )$$

The first number you put in parens is your starting number. Any numbers after that are the numbers you're subtracting from the first number.

JUGGLING YOUR FINANCES: BASIC EXCEL GUIDE

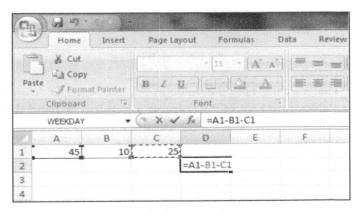

You can also combine the subtraction sign with the SUM function. So if you have two cells next to each other that you want to subtract from another number, you can write a formula like this:

$$=(\ ) - \text{SUM}(\ )$$

Where the value you start with is the number you want to subtract everything from and the cells in the SUM function parens are all the numbers you want to subtract from the first number.

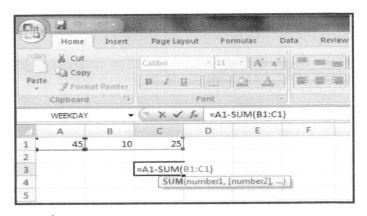

In the example above, see how the formula is:

=A1-SUM(B1:C1)

That's saying take the value in A1 and subtract from it the values in B1 and C1. You can, of course, expand that to include hundreds of values if you wanted.

So those are your two options for subtraction. Type a formula into one cell or create your own formula.

Pretty simple, really.

Now let's walk through some examples using the types of calculations you'll want to perform to get a handle on your finances.

SUBTRACTION: EXAMPLES

Example 1: How much money will be left after you pay your bills?

Let's use the numbers above and say that you have $5,963.63 in your accounts.
We already calculated that your expenses for the month were $1,125.
After you pay those bills, how much will you have left? $4,838.63.
How do we do find this in Excel?
Time for another piece of information. You can add or subtract values that are on different worksheets. (You can even do this across spreadsheets, but that gets into advanced work, so we're not going to go there right now.)
In this case, the $5,963.63 value is on our Assets worksheet and the $1,125 is on our Expenses worksheet.

Option 1:

Add more lines into the Assets worksheet and pull in the monthly expense amount from the Expenses worksheet in Row 7 and then perform subtraction in the Assets worksheet:

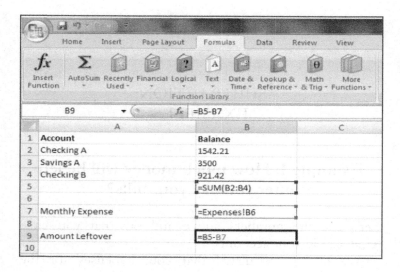

To do this, in cell B7 of the Assets worksheet, type:

=

And then navigate over to the Expenses worksheet, click on cell B6 which has the amount of total monthly expenses, and hit enter. This should give you the following formula in cell B7 of the Assets worksheet:

=Expenses!B6

That means that cell B7 in the Assets worksheet now has the same value as cell B6 in the Expenses worksheet.

Once you pull the value from the Expenses worksheet into the Assets worksheet, you can just use a simple subtraction formula in cell B9, to get the amount leftover:

$$=B5-B7$$

The screenshot above is set to show formulas, but normally it would just look like this:

	A	B	C	D	E	F	G
1	Account	Balance					
2	Checking A	$1,542.21					
3	Savings A	$3,500.00					
4	Checking B	$ 921.42					
5		$5,963.63					
6							
7	Monthly Expense	$1,125.00					
8							
9	Amount Leftover	$4,838.63					
10							

Option 2:

Put all of the information you want to work with into a new worksheet. (See Adding A New Worksheet in the tips and tricks section for how to have Excel add more than the three original worksheets you start with.)

In that new worksheet, you'd just type =, then go find the total assets value from the Assets worksheet, click on it, type -, and go find the total expenses value from the Expenses worksheet, and hit enter. That would give you the answer in one cell.

You could be more fancy and put labels for each value, list them in separate cells, and then use a basic formula to subtract the one from the other.

Here's what the two options look like in the same spreadsheet:

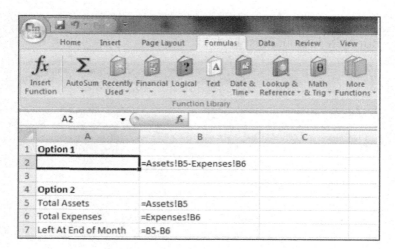

Note that I have the worksheet set to show formulas here. Normally you'd just see the numerical values in each cell.

Under Option1, the entire calculation is made in one cell. Under Option 2, the values are brought over from the other worksheets in cells B5 and B6 and then the calculation is made in cell B7.

Let's walk through that first formula for a minute:

=Assets!B5-Expenses!B6

That's saying take the value from cell B5 on the Assets spreadsheet and subtract from it the value from cell B6 on the Expenses spreadsheet.

In Excel, when it references a cell in a different worksheet than the one you're in, it lists the worksheet name followed by an exclamation sign before the cell number like you see above in cells B2, B5, and B6. When the referenced cells are in the current worksheet, then it just lists the cell numbers, like you see in cell B7 above.

Example 2: Your Net Worth

Your net worth is all of your assets minus all of your liabilities. It's basically a calculation of what you'd have left if you took everything you have and paid off everything you owe. We won't get into it here, but I find it a fairly worthless number. Liquid net worth is far more valuable in my opinion, but we'll calculate net worth anyway.

Same process as above. This time we take the total of all of your assets and subtract all of your liabilities.

You can do it in the Assets spreadsheet, the Liabilities spreadsheet, or a new one.

In this case, when I went to do it in a new worksheet, I realized I hadn't yet totaled all of the liabilities. Rather than back out of my formula, I just did the addition in the formula itself.

It ended up looking like this:

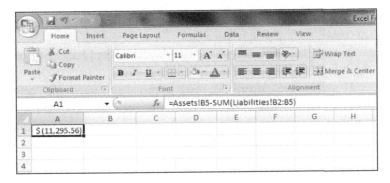

See the formula?

=Assets!B5-SUM(Liabilities!B2:B5)

Same as before, I typed in =, navigated to the Assets tab and clicked on cell B5 where the total value of my assets was, typed in the − sign, and then navigated to the Liabilities tab.

This is when I realized I had a problem.

So I clicked into the formula bar, deleted the word Liabilities!, replaced it with the word SUM and a left paren, and then highlighted the four cells I wanted to add, and finished with the closed paren. And I ended up with this:

=Assets!B5-SUM(Liabilities!B2:B5)

Excel put in the Liabilitites!B2:B5 part of the formula when I highlighted the cells.

If that's confusing, just make sure you have a summary value on both tabs. Then your formula will look something like this:

=Assets!B5-Liabilities!B6

Where cell B6 on the Liabilities worksheet contains the total of all the liabilities.

Notice that the answer is displayed as $ (11,295.56) or -11295.6. They mean the same thing.

If you see numbers in parens in a field, like $(11,295.56), that means the number is a negative number.

In this case, your net worth is negative about $11,000 because you owe more than you have. Not all that uncommon for many people, especially those just getting started.

Example 3: The Amount of Your Shortfall

You might've noticed that with the numbers we're using here, you are earning less than your monthly bills

In our example, you earned $182.23 in January but spent $1,125, which means a shortfall of $942.77. Fortunately, you had money in the bank to pay your bills, so you were actually able to pay them, but if you hadn't, that would've been how much more you needed to earn to pay everyone you owed.

To calculate the shortfall in Excel, find where you want to make the calculation, type in =, go to the Income worksheet, click on the cell with the total income for the month, type in the − sign, go to the Expenses worksheet, click on the cell with your total expenses for the period, and hit enter.

You should get $(942.77) or -942.77 depending on how you have the cell formatted. The formula will look something like this:

=Income!D9-Expenses!B6

Where D9 and B6 are the respective cells in each of the worksheets that have the total income and expenses for the period, and Income and Expenses are the names of the respective worksheets that contain the information.

* * *

There you have it. That's how you do subtraction in Excel. It should be obvious, but I'll say it anyway: You can use any formula in Excel across worksheets not just subtraction. If you want to add values that are in two different worksheets, you can. Or multiply them. Or divide them. Or any of the other many, many functions that Excel has.

Really, the best way to master Excel is to play in it. Set up different values and work with them until you're comfortable that you understand how it works and how the formulas should look.

Now on to multiplication.

MULTIPLICATION: OVERVIEW

Just like with subtraction, there are really only two ways to multiply values in Excel.

Option 1: Put The Entire Formula In A Cell

First, you can just enter the formula into any cell and hit enter.

Just as before, in Excel you need to START with the = sign.

(Now that we're far enough along, I'll confuse you a bit and let you know that you can also start with the + or - sign for formulas, but, really, I think using the = sign is more intuitive, so that's what I always recommend. Unless you're used to using HP calculators which I think do require use of the + or - sign before each number.)

Second, you use the * sign to indicate multiplication. (As opposed to a calculator which uses an x symbol.)

So, for example, if I wanted to multiply 3 times five, I could start typing in the cell I'm already in or left-click in a different cell and enter the following into the cell:

=3*5

When you hit enter, the cell should show you the value 15. If you then arrow back up to the cell you just used, you'll see the formula (=3*5) in the formula bar above the spreadsheet and the value (15) in the cell. Like so:

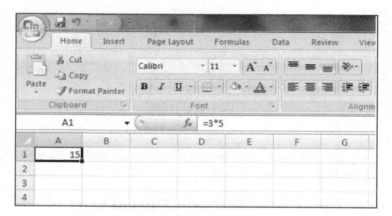

As above, remember that the Esc key and Ctrl+Z are your friends if something doesn't work the way you think it should. Just back up and try it again.

Option 2: Enter Your Own Formula

Again, sometimes this is the easiest way to do things. Multiplication works the same as subtraction. You just put the * sign between each of the cells you want to multiply.

So, the basic Excel formula for multiplying things is:

=()*()*()

Like this:

JUGGLING YOUR FINANCES: BASIC EXCEL GUIDE

In the example above, we're multiplying 2 times 3 times 4 to get 24. Except, as with addition and subtraction, we use the cell names not the actual numbers for our formula. So you get:

$$= A1*C1*E1$$

Note that with multiplication, you can put the numbers in any order you want.

No fancy shortcuts that I know of with multiplication. You have to manually enter or click on each cell you want to include in your formula and include the star sign between each of the numbers you're multiplying.

Now let's walk through some examples.

MULTIPLICATION: EXAMPLES

Example 1: How Much You'll Earn When You Know The Rate of Pay

Multiplication basically makes adding the same number over and over again easy. Which comes in handy if you have, for example, a job that pays an hourly wage.

Let's say you're trying to figure out the gross (so this is before taxes or anything else) amount that you'll earn at your new retail job. When they hired you they told you your hourly pay was going to be $8.25.

How much can you expect to earn next month if they give you twenty hours a week and there are four weeks in the month?

Well, multiply the amount you earn per hour ($8.25) times the number of hours you're going to work (20) times the number of weeks you'll work (4).

In Excel it will look something like this if you just input the formula:

$$=8.25*20*4$$

And the answer you get is 660.

Or you can put the values in their own cells and multiply them and get something that looks like this:

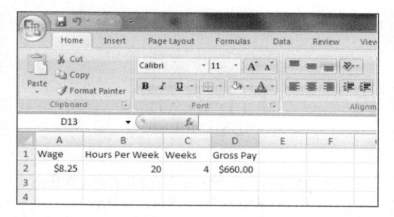

The formula for this using the screen above would be:

$$=A2*B2*C2$$

What if the answer doesn't make sense? What if you look at your result and think something must be wrong. You can click in the formula bar to see what cells were actually used in the formula and where each one was used.

For example, below I multiplied the values in cells A1, C1, and E1. When I click in the formula bar it highlights each value in a different color both in the formula bar and in the worksheet so that I can easily match them up and make sure that they were used where I wanted them to be used:

JUGGLING YOUR FINANCES: BASIC EXCEL GUIDE

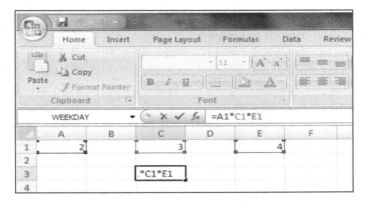

Doing this is an easy way to troubleshoot a formula that doesn't seem to be giving you the right result. (And, once again, I'll make an argument that you learn math well enough that you understand when an answer doesn't make sense. You're never going to double-check your work unless you know what you're doing well enough to understand that something isn't right. Excel is a great tool, but it's only as good as the person using it.)

Example 2: Calculating Your Net Earnings From Your Gross Earnings

Unless you're doing cash-based work, like housesitting, or you have an exemption from taxes, like certain individuals with very low incomes, or you're self-employed and expected to pay taxes yourself, chances are when you get paid it won't be the gross amount you earned.

It will be that amount minus some amount of taxes.

How much you lose to taxes depends on how much you make in that pay period and what you claim in terms of exemptions.

For simplicity's sake, let's assume that you make the same amount every pay period. Further, let's assume that you know what your take-home pay is on average compared to your gross income.

So, say you've done this. And you've figured out that for every dollar you earn, you actually get paid 82 cents.

That means that your take-home pay (or net pay) is 82% of your gross pay.

Now let's calculate what your actual take-home pay will be given various gross income amounts.

Let's say you know that you earn $8.25 an hour, there are 4 weeks in the month, and you want to know what you'll take home if you work 20 hours, 30 hours, 40 hours, 50 hours, or 60 hours per week.

Putting it in Excel, it might look something like this:

	A	B	C	D	E
1	Wage	Weeks			
2	$ 8.25	4			
3					
4	Hours Per	Gross Pay	% Takehome After Tax	Takehome Pay	
5	20	$ 660.00	82%	$ 541.20	
6	30	$ 990.00	82%	$ 811.80	
7	40	$ 1,320.00	82%	$1,082.40	
8	50	$ 1,650.00	82%	$1,353.00	
9	60	$ 1,980.00	82%	$1,623.60	
10					

Our given amounts are your wage, $8.25 per hour, and the number of weeks, 4, so I've put those at the top.

Next, in column A I've listed the various number of hours you might work. Next to that is our first calculation, your gross pay. That's A2 times B2 times each of the hours listed in cells A5 through A9.

In column C we've listed the amount of your pay that you get to take home after taxes, 82%. Now, we use column D to calculate your actual take-home pay for each number of hours worked per week. The formula in D5 looks like this:

JUGGLING YOUR FINANCES: BASIC EXCEL GUIDE

$$=C5*B5$$

What if you know your tax rate instead? In this case, 18%? Then you'd just need to combine subtraction and multiplication into the equation. If you know that your tax rate is 18% then you also know that what you take home from your gross pay is 100% minus 18%.

Instead of listing 82% in column C, we list 18% and label column C as tax rate. You can see the screenshot of this on the next page.

(Note that the row numbers are different than in the image above.)

The equation becomes:

$$=(1-C13)*B13$$

And here's what the spreadsheet looks like:

	A	B	C	D	E
1	Wage	Weeks			
2	$ 8.25		4		
3					
11					
12	Hours Per	Gross Pay	Tax Rate	Takehome Pay	
13	20	$ 660.00	18%	$ 541.20	
14	30	$ 990.00	18%	$ 811.80	
15	40	$ 1,320.00	18%	$1,082.40	
16	50	$ 1,650.00	18%	$1,353.00	
17	60	$ 1,980.00	18%	$1,623.60	

Note how (1-C13) is in parens. That's because otherwise Excel will do the calculations in the wrong order and, in this case, would multiply C13*B13 and then subtract it from 1. The parens tell it to do the subtraction first before any multiplication.

This works the same as what you learned in school about what order to do calculations in.

If that's too complex, you can always break it out so you calculate your taxes and then subtract those from your gross pay. Like this:

	A	B	C	D	E
1	Wage	Weeks			
2	8.25	4			
3					
18					
19	Hours Per Week	Gross Pay	Tax Rate	Taxes	Takehome Pay
20	20	=$A$2*A20*$B$2	0.18	=B20*C20	=B20-D20
21	30	=$A$2*A21*$B$2	0.18	=B21*C21	=B21-D21
22	40	=$A$2*A22*$B$2	0.18	=B22*C22	=B22-D22
23	50	=$A$2*A23*$B$2	0.18	=B23*C23	=B23-D23
24	60	=$A$2*A24*$B$2	0.18	=B24*C24	=B24-D24
25					

Combine the three and you get the following results:

	A	B	C	D	E	F
1	Wage	Weeks				
2	$ 8.25		4			
3						
4	Hours Per	Gross Pay	% Takehome After Tax	Takehome Pay		
5	20	$ 660.00	82%	$ 541.20		
6	30	$ 990.00	82%	$ 811.80		
7	40	$ 1,320.00	82%	$ 1,082.40		
8	50	$ 1,650.00	82%	$ 1,353.00		
9	60	$ 1,980.00	82%	$ 1,623.60		
10						
11						
12	Hours Per	Gross Pay	Tax Rate	Takehome Pay		
13	20	$ 660.00	18%	$ 541.20		
14	30	$ 990.00	18%	$ 811.80		
15	40	$ 1,320.00	18%	$ 1,082.40		
16	50	$ 1,650.00	18%	$ 1,353.00		
17	60	$ 1,980.00	18%	$ 1,623.60		
18						
19	Hours Per	Gross Pay	Tax Rate	Taxes	Takehome Pay	
20	20	$ 660.00	18%	$ 118.80	$ 541.20	
21	30	$ 990.00	18%	$ 178.20	$ 811.80	
22	40	$ 1,320.00	18%	$ 237.60	$ 1,082.40	
23	50	$ 1,650.00	18%	$ 297.00	$ 1,353.00	
24	60	$ 1,980.00	18%	$ 356.40	$ 1,623.60	

Same answer each time, the last one just breaks the steps out so that only one function is performed with each step.

Example 3: Your Annual Earnings or Expenses Based Upon One Period of Earnings or Expenses

Another way to use multiplication in managing your finances is to project how much money you'll earn or need for an entire year based upon how much you earn or need in a particular period such as a month.

Up above, we calculated that you would need $1,125 to pay your monthly expenses

If you know that your expenses will be the same for the entire year, how much will you need to cover all of those expenses?

Well, there are twelve months in a year so you need twelve times $1,125.

In Excel:

	A	B	C
1	Expense	Amount	Date Due
2	Rent	$ 500.00	1/1/2015
3	Car Insurance	$ 125.00	1/15/2015
4	Utilities	$ 75.00	1/23/2015
5	Credit Card	$ 425.00	1/16/2015
6		$ 1,125.00	
7			
8			
9	Annualized	$13,500.00	

You get $13,500.

And the formula in this case is:

$$= B6*12$$

Keep in mind, that if you're annualizing your expenses that's the amount you need to actually get paid. In other words, you need to take home at least $13,500.

So if you were offered a job that paid a salary of $13,500 it wouldn't be enough to cover your bills. You'd need to earn enough to not only pay your bills, but cover the amount of taxes that are taken out with each paycheck.

We can make the same type of calculation with your earnings.

We take what you earned this month and multiply it times 12 to get your annual income.

In the addition example, we had you earning $182.23 for the month. If you earned that every month for the next year, you would earn $2,186.76 for the year.

Next, you can combine your annual earnings and your annual expenses to determine how much you're going to be short (or have in excess if that's the case) for the entire year.

In this case, going back to subtraction, if you earn $2,186.76 and you spend $13,500, you will find yourself short $11,313.24.

* * *

So that's multiplication. On to division.

DIVISION: OVERVIEW

Just like with subtraction and multiplication, there are really only two ways to divide values in Excel.

Option 1: Put The Entire Formula In A Cell

First, you can just enter the formula into any cell and hit enter. Just as before, in Excel you need to START with the = sign.

In Excel you use the '/' sign to indicate division. (As opposed to ÷ on a calculator.)

So, for example, if I wanted to divide 15 by 5, I could start typing in the cell I'm already in or left-click on a different cell and enter the following:

$$=15/5$$

When you hit enter, the cell should show you the value 3. If you then arrow back up to the cell you just used, you'll see the formula, =15/5, in the formula bar above the worksheet and the value, 3, in the cell. Like so:

As above, remember that the Esc key and Ctrl+Z are your friends if something doesn't work the way you think it should. Just back up and try it again.

Option 2: Enter Your Own Formula

Again, sometimes the the easiest way to do things is to write the formula yourself.

Division works the same as subtraction. You just put the / sign between each of the cells you want to divide and start with the value that you want to divide into smaller pieces.

So, the basic Excel formula for dividing things is:

$$=(\ )/(\ )$$

Order matters with division, so be sure to put the number you want to divide first and the number you want to divide into it second.

Also, you really can only use two numbers for this unlike with multiplication, subtraction, and addition. (You could technically use parens to write a formula that divides more than two numbers, but it would get pretty messy pretty fast, so we're not going to go there.)

Here's an example of creating your own formula:

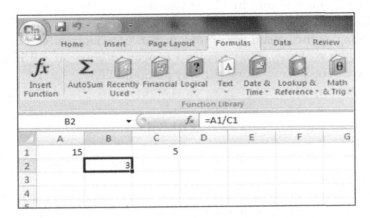

To create this, I just clicked in cell B2, typed =, clicked on cell A1, typed /, clicked on cell C1, and hit enter.

My result is 3 and the formula is:

$$=A1/C1$$

No fancy shortcuts that I know of. Just manually enter or click on each cell you want to include in your formula and include the slash sign between the numbers.

* * *

Note that for those of you eager to do something more complicated, you can use addition and subtraction on either side of that slash. So, I could add cells A1 and B1 together and then divide the total by cell C1.

If you do so, make sure to use your parens properly. Like this:

$$=(A1+B1)/C1$$

This way Excel knows to add A1 and B1 together and then divide the sum by C1. If you don't put the parens in the right place, then Excel is going to get the order wrong. (Once again, an argument for knowing math well enough to know what result to expect so you can tell if something isn't working the way it should be.)

If you enter:

$$=A1+B1/C1$$

Then Excel will divide B1 by C1 and then add that amount to A1.

Remember those math lessons from school? This is called the math order of operations if you want to research it further. Also, in Excel you can click on the little question mark in the top corner and search for Operator Precedence.

Basically, Excel calculates starting on the left side of the equation and moves to the right. Multiplication and division have precedence over addition and subtraction. So, Excel will go through an equation and do all multiplication and division starting on the left side and moving to the right. Then it'll go back through and do all addition and subtraction. Again moving from left to right.

Anything you put in parens gets calculated first regardless of whether it's addition, subtraction, multiplication, or division. (Within the parens, that order is followed again.)

So, Excel will go through an equation, do the parts in parens, and then go back to the beginning of the equation and start with multiplication/division.

If you're going to write complex formulas like this, be very comfortable with math and how it works. And if you are writing a new formula and want to be sure you did it right, use Excel to calculate each step separately and compare the final answer you get to your complex formula result. Work at it until you get the same answer both ways. AND make sure that that answer makes sense, that each step you took to get there is a logical step.

* * *

Okay, enough of that little digression. If you didn't follow it, don't worry. Not everyone will want to use complex formulas in their spreadsheets and you can manage your finances just fine without them. I just wanted to throw that in there for the few readers who are chomping at the bit to do something a little more complicated.

Now on to some examples of how to apply division to your finances.

DIVISION: EXAMPLES

Example 1: How Much You Earn or Spend on Average

Let's say you're trying to put together a budget, but there are certain things you do that aren't consistent. Maybe you housesit sometimes, but not on a regular schedule.

Should you just forget that income altogether? No.
What about using the most you earn each month? No.
What about the least? No.

If you consistently earn money from housesitting then you can use an average to figure out how much you normally earn from housesitting.

The more variation in the numbers, the trickier doing this becomes. Not from a math perspective. Math doesn't care. From a budgeting perspective. But right now we're just talking about basic math and how to use it, so we'll just calculate the average and assume that's accurate.

Let's walk through an example. Say you've been housesitting for six months now and you've earned the following amounts each month: $110, $200, $45, $80, $50, and $175. How much did you earn total for those six months?

$660. (110+200+45+80+50+175)

How much did you earn on average?

Well, take the total amount earned, $660, and divide it by the number of months in the sample. In this case, six.

In Excel it might look like this:

	A	B	C	D	E	F
1						
2	Month	Monthly Housesitting Income				
3	January	110				
4	February	200				
5	March	45				
6	April	80				
7	May	50				
8	June	175				
9		660		110		
10						

You have three options for how to calculate an average because Excel actually has a formula specific to averages and the bottom right corner of an Excel spreadsheet will also display the average. (As we noted in the addition section when we looked at that bottom corner for a quick sum of the cell values.)

Option 1:

Just type in the formula yourself. You can either use the total of the six cells that we already have in the spreadsheet and divide it by the number in the sample. In that case, your formula is:

$$=B9/6$$

Or, you can write a formula that sums the six values you want to average and divides them by the number of values in the sample. In that case, the formula is:

$$=SUM(B3:B8)/6$$

Either way, your answer should be 110.

Option 2:

You can use the AVERAGE function to take the average of the cells
The basic formula is:

$$=AVERAGE\ (\ )$$

Where you include in the parens the values you want to average. In this case, your specific formula is then:

$$=AVERAGE(B3:B8)$$

Note in the below image, that something isn't working right:

	A	B	C	D	E	F
1						
2	Month	Monthly Housesitting Income				
3	January	110				
4	February	200				
5	March					
6	April	80				
7	May	50				
8	June	175				
9		615	=$B$9/6	102.5		
10			=SUM($B$3:$B$8)/6	102.5		
11			=AVERAGE($B$3:$B$8)	123		

That's because if you have any months where you have a zero value, then you need to be very careful in using the average function. If you leave the cell blank, like I did above for March, Excel won't include that cell in the average. Instead of averaging six months of results, it will only average five months. Make sure to enter a value of zero in any cell that you want included in the average function.

Option 3:
You can highlight the six cells you want to average and see the value listed for average in the bottom right corner of the spreadsheet

Again, this one also doesn't work if you have any cells that are blank. You need to enter zero in those cells for them to be included.

* * *

Another note here. If you ever want to display the contents of a cell as text, you can just put a single quote at the start of the cell and Excel will treat it as text even if the next symbol in the cell is a -, +, or = sign which generally indicate a formula. That's what I did in cells C9 to C11 in that last screenshot.

Example 2: How Many Hours You Need to Work To Earn A Certain Gross Amount

Remember above when we determined that you had a bit of a shortfall between what you were spending and what you were earning? Well, you can use division to figure out how many hours you need to work per month to close that gap.

JUGGLING YOUR FINANCES: BASIC EXCEL GUIDE

Above we said you were earning $182.23, but that your expenses were $1,125 per month so your shortfall for the month was $942.77. We also said that you were paid $8.25 an hour at your job.

To figure out how many hours you need to work to make 942.77 you can just divide that amount by 8.25. But that's not going to tell you how many hours you actually need to work. To do that, you need to also account for taxes. Like this:

	A	B	C	D	E
1	Need to Take Home	942.77		942.77	
2					
3	Hourly Pay	8.25		8.25	
4	Net After Taxes	82%		82%	
5	Net Hourly Pay	6.765		=$B$3*$B$4	
6					
7	Hrs Needed	139.3599		=$B$1/$B$5	

First, we list the fixed values: How much you need to earn (cell B1), how much you earn per hour (cell B3), and how much you take home after taxes (cell B4)

Next, we calculate a net hourly pay in cell B5. (The formula is in cell D5.) This is basically saying that, given the amount you pay in taxes, you actually take home $6.77 per hour.

Finally, we can calculate how many hours you need to work based upon your net hourly pay to make that $942.77. That's in cell B7 with the formula showing in cell D7.

(Note that the above is one way to do that calculation. You could also take 942.77 divide it by 8.25 and then divide that by .82. It'll give you the same result.)

Example 3: How Much You Need to Gross In Order to Take Home A Certain Amount

Another way to approach this problem is to figure out how much you need to gross in order to make enough to meet the shortfall.

So, how do you calculate the actual amount you need to earn in order to be able to take home $942.77?

You can use division and the estimated percent of your pay that you take home.

So, if $942.77 is what you need to take home, there's a number out there (the gross pay) that when it's multiplied by the percent of your pay that you actually receive (82% in our example from above) will give you $942.77.

That's $A \times B = C$.

If you know C and A, then you can calculate B. Solve the equation above for B and you get $B=C/A$. So, if you divide C by A you'll know how much you need to earn.

Here's what that approach looks like. In cell B22 we are dividing C (amount you need to take home) by A (amount you receive after taxes). The formula used is in cell D22.

You can see that in cell B14 the formula is a little different because we used 1 minus the tax rate instead of the net after taxes.

JUGGLING YOUR FINANCES: BASIC EXCEL GUIDE

	A	B	C	D	E
11	Need to Take Home	942.77		942.77	
12	Tax Rate	18%		18%	
13	Hourly Pay	8.25		8.25	
14	Need to Gross	1149.72		=$B$11/(1-$B$12)	
15	Hours to Work	139.3599		=$B$14/$B$13	
16					
17	OR				
18					
19	Need to Take Home	942.77		942.77	
20	Net After Taxes	82%		82%	
21	Hourly Pay	8.25		8.25	
22	Need to Gross	1149.72		=$B$17/$B$18	
23	Hours to Work	139.3599		=$B$14/$B$21	

Either way, we get $1,149.72, which is the amount you'll gross if your work the 139.36 hours we calculated before.

Example 4: How Many Months of Expenses You Can Cover with the Current Amount of Cash In the Bank

This one is pretty simple compared to the others, but very handy to know if you're spending more than you're earning.

How do you do it?

Take the amount you have in the bank and divide by how much you spend each month.

Like this:

	A	B	C	D	E	F
1	Account	Balance				
2	Checking A	$1,542.21				
3	Savings A	$3,500.00				
4	Checking B	$ 921.42				
5		$5,963.63				
6						
7	Monthly Expense	$1,125.00				
8						
9	Months Covered	5.30				

Handy number to know. (And ideally 3 or above, but many people don't manage that.)

If nothing else, when managing your finances try to keep this number greater than 1 so you know you have this month's expenses covered no matter what happens.

* * *

Alright. That's it. That's basic math using Excel.

Of course, there's a lot more to using Excel than just those four functions. That's what the next section covers on a basic level.

If there's something you want to do that isn't covered in this guide, try searching Excel's help function. It's actually pretty good. And if not, try the web.

EXCEL FORMATTING AND NAVIGATION TIPS AND TRICKS

I tried to keep the earlier sections of this guide limited to how to perform basic mathematical functions in Excel, but if you're going to spend any amount of time working in Excel then you need to learn how to format cells and navigate your way around.

That's what this section is for. It's an alphabetical listing of different things you might want to do.

Adding a New Worksheet

As I mentioned above, when you open a new Excel file, you'll have three worksheets that you can use named Sheet 1, Sheet 2, and Sheet 3.

If you need more than three worksheets (like I seem to whenever I create a new Excel file), simply click on the fourth tab at the bottom of the screen. The one that has a symbol on it that looks like a mini worksheet with a yellow star in the top left corner. Excel will then insert a new worksheet.

Auto-Suggested Text

If you've already typed text into a cell, Excel will suggest that text to you in subsequent cells in the same column.

For example, if in cell A1, you type STAR, when you go to A2 and type an S, Excel will automatically suggest to you STAR. If you don't want to use the text, then keep typing. If you do, then hit enter.

There are a few times when auto-suggested text doesn't appear. One is when there are too many empty cells between the one that you already completed and the one you're now completing. Another is if you have a very long list that you've completed and the matching entry is hundreds of rows away from the one you're now completing.

Excel will also only make a suggestion if there is a unique match to what you've already typed. So if you have Star 1 and Star 2 in your spreadsheet and type an S, Excel won't make a suggestion.

It also doesn't make suggestions for numbers, only text or text/number combinations.

JUGGLING YOUR FINANCES: BASIC EXCEL GUIDE

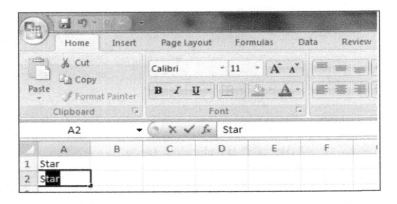

Auto-suggested text can be very handy to use if you have to enter one of a limited number of choices over and over again and can't easily copy the information from cell to cell.

Another tip: In situations where you want to enter similar, but not identical information, (for example in the Liabilities example we had Student Loan A and Student Loan B), you can use the auto-suggested text and then change it. So, after we entered Student Loan A, when we typed an S, it should have suggested Student Loan A to us. At that moment, if you hit F2 and use the right arrow Excel will take you to the end of the text and then you can just backspace and change the A to a B. Saves having to retype the whole phrase.

F2 can be very handy in general.

Bolding Text

You do this by highlighting the cells you want bolded and clicking on the large capital B in the font section on the Home tab.

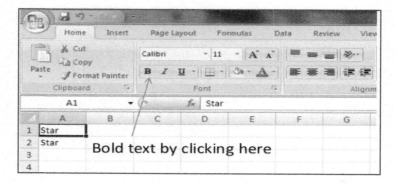

OR by highlighting the cells and hitting Ctrl+B. (That means hold down the key marked Ctrl and the b key at the same time.)

You can also bold part of the text in a cell by clicking into the cell, highlighting the portion of the text that you want to bold, and then either clicking on the large capital B in the Font section or hitting Ctrl+B.

Complex Math Functions

Any math whizzes reading this may have realized that you can pretty much put any mathematical function into Excel as long as you get your parens in the right place.

You want to multiply two numbers together, subtract something from that value, and then divide by another value? Go for it. The formula looks something like this:

$$=((A1*B1)-C1)/D1$$

Copying the Contents of One Cell To Another

This is very easy. Highlight the information you want to copy and hold down the Ctrl+C keys (so Ctrl and c at the same time). Go to the cell where you want to put the information you copied and hit Enter. If you want to copy to more than one location, instead of hitting Enter, hold down the Crtl+V keys (So Ctrl and v at the same time).

If you use Ctrl+V, you'll see that the original cell you copied from is still surrounded by a dotted line. If you're actually done and want to do something else, just hit the Esc key to get rid of the dotted line and keep going.

You can also right-click and select Copy from the dropdown menu and then right-click Paste from the dropdown menu in the cell where you want the information.

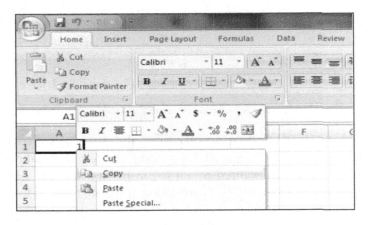

Copying Formatting From One Cell To Another

If you've formatted one cell the way you want it, you can use the format sweeper (that's what I call it because it looks like a broom to me, Microsoft calls it the Format Painter) to apply your format to all the cells you want it to apply to.

How does the format sweeper work? Let's say you entered all your information and formatted the first row the way you want all the rows to look, but then you entered information for the remaining rows and they aren't formatted properly. You just highlight the first row, click on the little broom in the top left corner that says Format Painter next to it, and then highlight the other rows you want formatted the same way. Excel will take the formatting from the first row and apply it to the other rows.

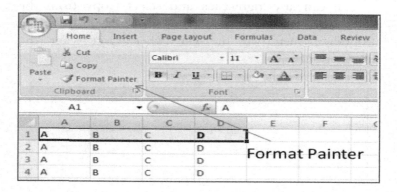

You need to be careful using the format sweeper because it will change all formatting in your destination cells. So, if you wanted a cell to be bolded but the one you choose to sweep the formatting from isn't, you'll lose the bold formatting. (I find this is more of a problem when using the tool in Word than in Excel, but it's still something to watch out for especially if you have borders around cells.)

Also, the tool will apply formatting to whatever cell you highlight next, which can be a problem if the cells you want to format aren't right next to the one you try to format sweep from.

In other words, do not use the arrow keys to navigate. Use your mouse or trackpad.

You need to click on the Format Painter and then immediately click on the cell(s) you want formatted that way.

It can also be particular if you select multiple cells to sweep the formatting from, so always check to see if the changes look right after you're done.

One more tip. If you double-click the format sweeper you can then apply the format to multiple selections. It will keep sweeping the format to all the cells you select until you click on the format sweeper again. Play around with it, you'll see what I'm talking about.

Copying Formulas To Other Cells While Keeping One Value Fixed

If you have a formula in cell C1, let's say it's A1+B1, and you copy it to cell C2, the formula will change so that it's now adding cells A2 and B2. This can be incredibly useful if you want to copy the same formula down multiple rows.

But sometimes you want to copy a formula while keeping the value of one of the cells fixed. To do this, you use the $ sign.

Let's say I want to see the various amounts I can earn if I work different hours per week, but my pay rate and the number of weeks in a month are constant. I can create a spreadsheet where my pay rate and number of weeks per month are fixed values displayed at the top of the spreadsheet.

I can then write a formula that always refers to those cells with the wage and weeks values.

Like this:

	A	B
1	Wage	Weeks
2	8.25	4
3		
4	Hours Per Week	Gross Pay
5	20	=$A$2*A5*$B$2
6	30	=$A$2*A6*$B$2
7	40	=$A$2*A7*$B$2
8	50	=$A$2*A8*$B$2
9	60	=$A$2*A9*$B$2

See the formula in cell B5. It was originally:

$$=A2*A5*B2$$

So, $8.25 per hour, times 20 hours, times 4 weeks. I then went back to that formula and inserted dollar signs before the letter and the number for cells A2 and B2. This locks the formula to using those two cells no matter where it's copied and pasted to.

Now, when I copy the formula down to the other rows below it, you can see that the formula continues to reference cells A2 and B2 even while the middle value changes for each row I'm copying to.

If you only want to keep the column the same, you just put the $ sign in front of the letter. ($A1).

If you only want to keep the row the same, you just put the $ sign in front of the number. (A$1).

Like this example where we're looking at different possible pay rates:

JUGGLING YOUR FINANCES: BASIC EXCEL GUIDE

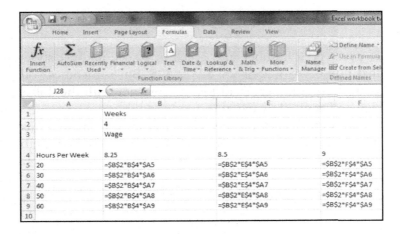

See how B2 is locked in ($B$2) for all cells, but only row 4 is locked in for the wages (B$4, E$4, F$4) and only column A is locked in for hours ($A5, $A6, etc.)? I wrote the formula once in cell B5 and then was able to just copy and paste it to the other cells.

If you don't have formulas showing like I do above, it looks like this:

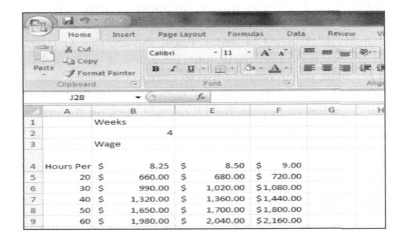

Currency Formatting

If you type a number into a cell in Excel, it'll just show that number. So, 25 is 25. $25 is $25. But sometimes you want those numbers to display as currency with the dollar sign and cents showing, too.

To do this, click on the cell(s) you want formatted this way, and then go to the Number section of the home tab and choose the $ sign.

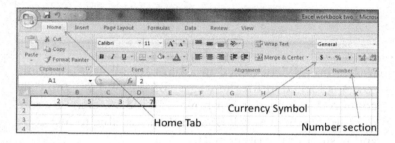

Date formatting

Sometimes Excel has a mind of its own about how to format dates. For example, I typed in 1/1 meaning January 1st. When I hit enter, Excel showed this as 1-Jan. It means the same thing, but I wanted it to look like 1/1/2015, which means I had to change the formatting.

To do this, click on the cell with your date in it, go to the Number section on the Home tab, click on the arrow next to the word Custom, and choose Short Date from the dropdown menu.

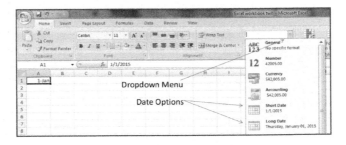

OR you can right click on the cell with the date in it and choose format cells from the dropdown menu.

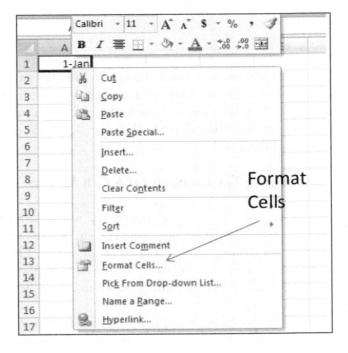

Next choose Date and then select the type of date format you want.

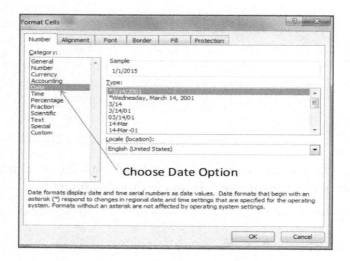

Note that if you just enter a month and day of the month like I did above, Excel will default to the current year. In my example above where it showed 1-Jan in the cell, Excel stored that date as January 1, 2015 even though it didn't show it.

Displaying The Contents Of A Cell As Text

Excel will try to turn the contents of a cell into a formula if you start with a negative sign, equals sign, or plus sign. It will also sometimes turns text describing a date into a formatted date. So, for example, December 15, displays as 15-Dec and Excel stores the information as December 15 of the current year.

To keep Excel from doing this, you can type a single quote mark before the contents of the cell. If you do so, Excel will display in the cell everything you typed as you typed it except for the single quote mark and will treat the contents of that cell as text.

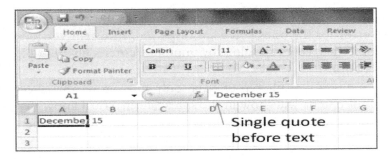

F2

If you click in a cell and hit the F2 key, this will take you to the end of the contents of the cell. This can be very useful when you need to edit the contents of a cell or to work with a formula in that cell.

Filtering Information

As long as you've set your data up with the first row used to label each column and the remaining rows to display the data, you can use filtering.

For example, in the Income tab above, you had three sources of income, Housesitting, Day Job, and Dogwalking. If you wanted to only see entries related to Housesitting, you could filter the information.

To filter, click on any of the cells in the first row and in the top right corner select Sort & Filter and then Filter. When you do this, gray arrows will show up next to each of the cells in the first row.

If you click on the arrow for any given column it should list all values in that column and you can choose which criteria to filter by. (The more recent the version of Excel, the better this list is and the more options you have for how to filter it.)

Once you have the dropdown menu, just check the boxes for the ones you want displayed. In recent versions of Excel you can filter by multiple criteria in multiple columns.

When you filter your data, only those rows that meet your criteria will show in the spreadsheet. You'll know that you've filtered the spreadsheet because the row numbers will be colored blue.

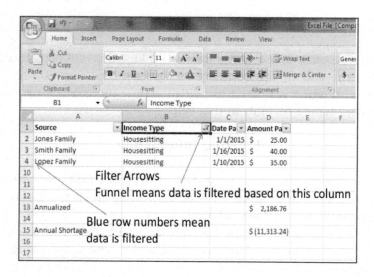

Sometimes it can be hard to tell what filter has been applied to a spreadsheet and annoying to try to go through each column and remove the filters. The easy way around this is to go back to Sort & Filter and choose Clear from the dropdown menu.

Formatting More Than One Cell At Once

This is easy. Just highlight all the cells you want formatted one way and change them all at once using the options on the Home tab or right-clicking and using the Format Cells option. (You can even highlight an entire column or row and do this, but if you do, try not to put in borders or shading, it looks weird because it continues for thousands of rows or hundreds of columns. I think it also affects your file size, too.)

Insert a Cell in a Worksheet

See below for how to insert an entire row or column. Sometimes you just want to insert one cell in the worksheet. In this case, click on where you want to insert the cell, right-click, and select Insert.

You'll be given four choices, Shift Cells Right, Shift Cells Down, Entire Row, Entire Column. (As you can see, the last two choices actually let you insert an entire row or column, although I don't think I've ever done that using these options.)

Shift Cells Right will insert your cell by moving every other cell in that row to the right. Shift Cells Down will insert your cell by moving every other cell in that column down. Be sure that the option you choose makes sense given the other data you've already entered in the worksheet.

Insert a Column or Row

Sometimes you'll enter information and then realize that you want to add a row or column right in the midst of the data you've already entered. If this happens, highlight the row or column where you want your new row or column to go, right-click, and select Insert. By highlight, I mean click on either the letter of the column or the number of the row. If you click on a cell in the worksheet, Excel will think you want to insert one cell instead of a whole row or column, but as you can see above, you can still insert a row or column using that option.

Moving Across a Row

You can either use the arrow keys (right to move right, left to move left) or the tab key (tab to move right, shift+tab to move left) to move across a row. If you enter information and hit enter, it will generally move you down one row, which isn't really what you want when you're inputting a set of information across a row, so arrows or the tab key are your friend and often a better choice than Enter.

Moving the Contents of a Cell

This is similar to copying the contents of a cell, but instead of using Ctrl+C or selecting Copy from the dropdown menu, you use Ctrl+X or select Cut from the dropdown menu. Once you reach the cell where you want to move the information you can hit Enter in the destination cell or Ctrl+V.

With formulas, cutting and moving the cell will keep the contents of the formula the exact same. So if you're formula was =A2+B2 it will still be =A2+B2. Whereas with Copy the formula will change based upon the number of rows and columns you've moved. If this doesn't make sense to you, just try it. Use Ctrl+C to copy a formula and move it to a different cell. Then use Ctrl+V to copy the same formula and move it to a different cell. Look at the resulting formulas and you'll see what I mean.

Paste Special

Sometimes you want to copy information in your worksheet but you don't want to copy everything about the cell. I most commonly do this when I want to copy the results of a calculation without copying the formula itself. Start the copying process the same by selecting your cell(s) and typing Ctrl+C, but instead of using Ctrl+V or Enter in the destination cell, right click in the cell and select Paste Special from the dropdown men. A box will pop up with a series of choices.

To just copy the result of a formula without copying the formula, choose Values.

Transpose is another nice option. It lets you take values you have in a column and paste them across a row or vice versa.

Renaming A Worksheet

The default name for worksheets in Excel are Sheet 1, Sheet 2, and Sheet 3. They're not very useful names for much of anything and if you have information in more than one worksheet, you're going to want to rename the worksheets to something that means something to you.

If you double left-click on a worksheet name (on the tab at the bottom) it will highlight in black and you can delete the name and name it whatever you want.

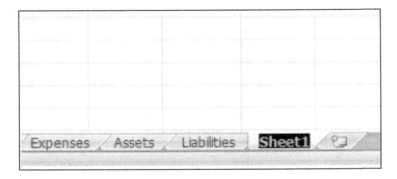

Well, almost whatever you want. There are limits to how long the name can be and what characters you use, but Excel will let you know if you mess it up.

Save Backups

If you're trying to create a new worksheet and you're experimenting to get things to work just right, don't be afraid to save multiple copies of the file. Once you have something working, save a copy. Work on the next thing. Save a new copy when you have part of it working. Work on the next thing. Save. Etc. At the end you can either delete the draft copies or save them for some point down the road when you figure out you messed something up somewhere and need to backtrack.

Just be sure if you do this that you name your files in a way that lets you know which one is the most recent version. For example, I'll call a file ABC File Draft 20150123. And when I save a new version the next day it becomes ABC File Draft 20150124. I know that the first file is the version I was working on on January 23rd and the second is the draft I was working on on January 24th.

A quick point here. Note how I wrote those dates? Year—Month—Day? (2015—01—23) There's a reason for that. When you sort your files by name, writing your dates in this format will result in the files being sorted in date order. If you write your dates as January 23 2015 then when you sort by name it does it alphabetically based upon the name of the month. Not very helpful but people do it all the time.

Sorting

If you've entered a lot of information into a worksheet and now want it to appear in a specific order, such as by date, you can sort it. For example, in the Expenses tab I entered due dates for bills, but if you look closely, the bills weren't in order of due date. Generally, I'd want that list sorted by date order so I could go down the list as the month progresses and check off each bill as it's paid.

To sort your data, select all columns that contain your information (otherwise, you'll sort part of your data and not sort the rest and then it won't match up properly), click on Sort & Filter in the top right corner of the Home tab, choose Custom Sort, and then choose to sort by the column you want to use to determine the order of your data.

You can actually sort by multiple columns in recent versions of Excel. Just choose to Add Level and then select your second sort criteria from the dropdown.

If you have information below your data that you don't want to sort, just highlight the cells with the data that you want to sort and leave out those other rows.

You can also right-click on the header row (so row 1 of whichever column you want to sort by) and choose Sort from the dropdown menu and then choose the option you want. (Which can include Custom Sort.) I find that this sometimes works without a problem, but sometimes the sort doesn't choose the cells that I think it should have. Be very careful if you have any empty rows or columns in your data. Chances are the right-click and Sort option will not work under those circumstances.

Your best bet is to play around with it a bit and watch what happens. Don't be afraid to hit Ctrl+Z and try it again if it doesn't do what you want.

If you have column names and in the Custom Sort option they aren't listed as options for your sort, make sure that the little box in the top right-hand corner that says "my data has headers" is checked.

You can also sort by going to the Data tab and choosing sort from there.

Undo

With any of the steps above (or below) don't be afraid to try things and then undo them if they don't work the way you expect them to. Ctrl+Z is your friend. Sometimes you need Ctrl+Z and then Esc to really clear whatever it was you were trying.

Don't be afraid to use Ctrl+Z. I use it all the time. I do something, think "that's not what I wanted", hit Ctrl+Z and try again. Honestly, the best way to learn Excel is through a little trial and error. Otherwise you'll always be stuck with what someone else showed you.

And if you go a little too far? Then re-do using Ctrl+Y.

Widening Columns

If the columns aren't as wide as you want, you have three options:

1. Right-click on the column and choose Column Width from the dropdown menu. When the box showing you the current column width appears, enter a new column width that is larger than the current width.
2. Place your cursor to the right side of the column until it looks like a line with arrows on either side. Left-click and hold, move the cursor to the right until the column is as wide as you want it to be.
3. Place your cursor on the right side of the column until it looks like a line with arrows on either side and double left-click. This will make the column as wide as the widest text currently in that column.

And if they end up too wide, then use Steps 1 or 2 to make the column more narrow.

Wrap Text

Sometimes you want to read all of the text in a cell, but you don't want that column to be too wide. If there isn't any content in the column next to the cell, Excel will automatically display the full contents, as you can see in cell A1 below.

As soon as there is content in the next column, like with cell A2 below where cell B2 has the text "ABC" in it, the contents of the cell that are displayed are limited to the column width.

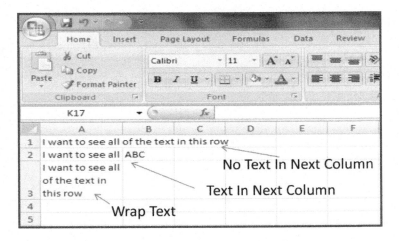

The solution to this is to use the Wrap Text option. This takes the text and places it on multiple lines so you can see all of it. (Note that Excel does have a limit as to how many rows of text it will display in one cell, so if you have any cells with lots of text in them, check to make sure that the full contents of the cell are visible.)

To use Wrap Text, select the cells containing the text you want to wrap, go to the middle of the Home Tab, and click on the Wrap Text option in the Alignment section.

Or, you can right-click on the cell, choose Format Cells from the dropdown menu, got to the Alignment tab and choose Wrap text under Text Control.

CONCLUSION

So there you have it.

There are any number of other tricks you can learn in Excel. Things like Pivot Tables, for example, can be incredibly handy for anyone who is self-employed and has multiple clients or products and wants to analyze that information.

But, honestly, the spreadsheet I use to track my finances on a regular basis pretty much uses addition, subtraction, multiplication, and division. I don't even use filtering in that one.

So this should've given you the basic foundation you need to move forward and get a handle on what you earn, what you spend, what you own, and what you owe, which are really the building blocks you need to juggle your finances and avoid a downhill slide into bankruptcy or financial ruin.

Note I didn't say to avoid debt. There are many times in life when debt is useful and valuable. You have to handle it correctly, but taking on student loan debt is how I was able to have the career and life I've had. I had no ability to get there without being willing to incur debt. None.

Anyway. That's a discussion for another guide.

I hope you learned a lot and learned enough to do the basic calculations and formatting you're going to need.

Good luck!

ABOUT THE AUTHOR

M.L. Humphrey is a former stockbroker with a degree in Economics from Stanford and an MBA from Wharton who has spent close to twenty years as a regulator and consultant in the financial services industry.

You can reach M.L. at mlhumphreywriter@gmail.com or at mlhumphrey.com.

Made in the USA
Middletown, DE
11 November 2022